THEN AND THERE SERIES

General Editors:

Marjorie Reeves, M.A., Ph.D., and Paule Hodgson, M.A.

SAMUEL PEPYS IN LONDON

By

ELEANOR I. MURPHY, M.A.

Illustrations drawn from contemporary sources by
DUDLEY JARRETT

LONGMAN

LONGMAN GROUP LIMITED
London

*Associated companies, branches and representatives
throughout the world*

*First published 1958
Eighth impression 1973*

ISBN 0 582 20385 6

Acknowledgments

For permission to include line drawings based on copyright sources we
are indebted to the following: Central Museum, Northampton—page 44;
Horniman's Museum—pages 52 (right) and 54 (top); Master and
Fellows of Magdalene College, Cambridge—pages 3 and 33; National
Maritime Museum—pages 14, 22, 24 and 40; The Rector of St. Olave
Hart Street—pages 59 and 60; Sudley Art Gallery and Museum—page
32; The Society of Antiquaries—page 71; Victoria and Albert Museum
(Crown Copyright)—pages 31, 32 and 54 (foot).

*Printed in Hong Kong by
Peninsula Press Ltd*

CONTENTS

TO THE READER

WE do not know exactly how Samuel Pepys pronounced his name, but it is usually said as "peeps". It may be, however, that it was pronounced as if it were "peps" or "peppis".

If you look at a printed copy of the Diary kept by Samuel Pepys, you will notice that each year begins with a double date like this 1659/1660. (Can you see this in the reproduction of the actual diary on page 3?). This is because, at the time Pepys was writing, there were two ways of counting the years. Most countries in Europe began counting the New Year from January 1st, as we do now, but in England at that time the New Year was counted from March 25th. So, for example, between January 1st and March 25th a Frenchman would have said that it was 1660, while an Englishman would have said that it was still 1659. Pepys showed this by writing both figures down. In this book, whenever there is a double date, we have reckoned the year from January 1st.

All the illustrations in this book are either drawings of things actually used in those days, or drawings from pictures painted at that time. So the portraits show you people as they really were, and you can see for yourselves the things they saw and used.

SAMUEL PEPYS DECIDES TO KEEP A DIARY

IT was on January 1st, 1660, that Samuel Pepys began to keep a diary. He was 26 years old, he had a pretty young wife called Elizabeth, he lived in London, and he worked as a clerk in a government office.

We do not know why Pepys decided to start a diary. It is always interesting to keep a diary of your own, and to read it again years afterwards and be reminded of all sorts of things you have forgotten in the meantime—what you thought of a friend when you first met him, or what you used to like to do best when you were younger. Pepys must have felt that he would like to do something like that. Perhaps, since it was January 1st, he was thinking about the year ahead and wondering what lay in store for him, and then he decided that it would be interesting if, in future, he wrote down each evening before he went to bed something about what had happened to him during the day.

January 1st in 1660 fell on a Sunday, so in the evening when Pepys took a new notebook and wrote his day's news in it, he said that he had been to church, that they had had turkey for dinner—and that Elizabeth had burnt her hand in getting it ready—and after dinner they had gone to visit his father.

Samuel Pepys

Pepys kept his diary for nine years. Sometimes, if he was very tired at night and did not want to spend too long over it, or if nothing very exciting had happened that day, he would just write a short sentence like "This morning we met at the office: I dined at my house." If, however, it had been an interesting day, then he would write pages. In the years in which he was keeping his diary some unusually interesting things *did* happen in London.

Charles II came back from exile, so that there was a king on the throne again. There was a terrible outbreak of the plague in 1665 in which thousands of people died. The Great Fire burnt down the greater part of London in 1666. As Pepys was living in London when all this happened, he wrote long accounts of them in his diary each evening. Of course, such events did not happen every day, and Pepys would often write about the new suit he had bought or what Elizabeth was doing in the house, about what they had for dinner or what he had done in his spare time.

By 1669, Pepys had filled six note-books with the news of what had been happening to him each day in those nine years. His eyes, however, were beginning to hurt him a great deal. He had so much writing to do in his office, and he liked to read until so late at night, that he was afraid that he might go blind if he did not rest his eyes. So on May 31st, 1669, he wrote the last entry in his diary. He said that he could no longer see well enough to write it for himself, and so he would not be able to keep a diary any more. His eyes got better after he had had a holiday, and Pepys was able to return to work, but he never started the diary again. The six note-books which he filled from 1660 until 1669 are all that we have.

Pepys wrote the diary in shorthand, which looked like this:

Sometimes he wrote a sentence in French or Latin, Spanish or Greek. He used shorthand, not so much for secrecy as for speed, but it had the advantage that if his wife or any of his friends came across the diary in his room, they would not be able to understand it. It was, however, quite an easy shorthand that he used, and once the diaries had been noticed among his books many years later, it was a fairly simple matter to read what Pepys had written and to write it all out in longhand. This was done by a clergyman about a hundred years ago.

It is intriguing to get the chance of reading someone else's diary, because it tells us not merely what was happening at the time the diary was written, but also what that person thought about it all. For example, we should have known about the Great Fire of London in 1666 anyway: but Pepys' diary tells us exactly what it felt like to live through that week when London was burning. Then, too, it is usually easy to find out what happened in the past to important people: to kings and queens and famous people of the time. But it is much harder to find out what it was like for ordinary people like ourselves: what their homes were like, and what they did during the day at work or at home in the evenings for amusement. Many other people were keeping diaries at the same time as Pepys was writing his. John Evelyn, who was a friend of Pepys, kept one which has become famous, too. But none of the other diarists mentioned so many homely little details about everyday life as Pepys did in his.

This book, then, is about some of the things we know today because a young clerk called Samuel Pepys decided to begin a diary in 1660 and kept it for the next nine years as he lived and worked in London.

THE KING RETURNS TO ENGLAND

SAMUEL PEPYS was born on February 23rd, 1633, and so he grew up in very troubled times, for he was only nine years old when Civil War broke out between King Charles I and his Parliament in 1642. By the time Cromwell had defeated the King, Pepys was a sixteen-year old schoolboy at St. Paul's School in London. He was in the great crowd which stood in Whitehall on January 30th, 1649, to watch the execution of the King on a scaffold in front of the Banqueting Hall of the Palace of Whitehall. He was not one of those who hated the sight, for some of his relations were friends and neighbours of Oliver Cromwell, and so at that time Pepys was on Cromwell's side and not on the King's. Later on, he was bitterly ashamed of the fact that when he got back to school that day he had said that he was glad the King had been executed.

As he grew up, Pepys, like many other Englishmen, began to hate the *Commonwealth*.[1] Cromwell, whom he admired, died in 1658, and after that there was a struggle for power between leaders of the army whom few liked or respected. Even those men who had fought against Charles I began to wish that the Commonwealth were ended and that there could be a king in England once more. When Pepys began his diary on January 1st in 1660, no one knew what was going to happen. Whenever Pepys went to a tavern or a coffee-house he overheard

[1] You will find words printed like *this* in the Glossary on page 92.

5

men saying that they wished the King were back. Most men said quite openly that if only there could be a new Parliament elected freely, it would ask Charles I's son, who was then in exile in Holland, to come back to England to be King once more. There were great rejoicings when one of the army commanders, General Monk, marched south from Scotland with his army and took charge of London, saying that he would see that a free Parliament was called.

Pepys saw Monk leaving the Guildhall on February 11th, 1660, after Monk had said this to the Lord Mayor and Aldermen. Everyone in the streets was cheering General Monk and shouting "God bless your Excellence". That night, as Pepys walked in the City,

General Monk

he said there were bonfires everywhere: he counted seven or eight in one short street alone. Bells were ringing, and crowds were marching around the streets, shouting and cheering at the news. "It was past imagination", wrote Pepys that night. Londoners felt very glad that the Commonwealth was over, and that the King would almost certainly be coming back to England once more.

The new Parliament *did* ask the King to return, and on May 1st the King's reply was read out to Parliament. In it he promised to return and to forgive everyone who had fought against him and his father: the only people he would not forgive were the men who had condemned his father to death. Apart from that, he left everything to be settled by Parliament. This news, wrote Pepys in his diary on the following day, caused "great joy all yesterday at London, and at night more bonfires than ever, and ringing of bells, and drinking of the King's health upon their knees in the streets", which, despite his own excitement at the news, he said "methinks is a little too much."

Pepys did not see this rejoicing himself, for at the time it happened, he was away at sea with the fleet. He had an important cousin who was a Commander of the Fleet. This cousin, Sir Edward Montagu, had been a friend and supporter of Oliver Cromwell, but he hated the men who had tried to rule after Cromwell's death. So he was now one of those who wanted the King to return. He took Pepys to sea with him as his secretary in March, 1660. When Sir Edward and the officers of the fleet wrote to Charles to say that they would be loyal to him, it was Pepys who took the letter to the ship that carried it to Holland. When Charles wrote back to thank them for their promise of loyalty, Pepys wrote the reply for his cousin.

King Charles II

Then, more exciting still, the fleet sailed for Holland in May to bring the King back to England. There were great preparations as the ships crossed the sea. The harps which the Commonwealth had placed on a blue shield in the centre of the Union Flag, were replaced by a crowned C.R.; and the painters were set to work to decorate once again the ships' sterns with the Royal Arms. All the

8

officers got new suits, or had their best suits trimmed with ribbons, so that everyone would look his best when the King came on board. Here are the Royal Arms, supported, as they are today, by the lion and the unicorn:

When the King, with his brothers the Duke of York and the Duke of Gloucester, came down to the quay, all the guns fired a salute to welcome him and the ships were gay with *pennants*. Pepys wanted to share in the excitement of welcoming the King, so he fired a gun near his cabin and almost shot himself. However, he was not hurt and he was ready to enjoy the scene when the Royal party came on board his ship.

The first thing the King did was to rename the ships, for they still had the names which the Commonwealth government had given them. The ship the King had boarded was called the NASEBY after one of the battles in which his father had been defeated in the Civil War. This the King changed to THE CHARLES. Another of the ships he called THE HAPPY RETURN. When all the party was on board the ships, Pepys wrote, "we weighed anchor, and with a fresh gale and most happy weather we set sail for England."

On the voyage, the King was friendly to everyone. He told some of them—and Pepys was among his listeners—of all his adventures since his father had been executed. He told them how he had been defeated by Cromwell at the battle of Worcester in 1651, and then had wandered, disguised as a servant, until he could escape from England to France. Pepys wrote: "it made me ready to weep to hear the stories that he told of his difficulties that he had passed through, as his travelling four days and three nights on foot, every step up to his knees in dirt, with nothing but a green coat and a pair of country breeches on, and a pair of country shoes that made him so sore all over his feet, that he could scarce stir."

Those unhappy days were now over for the King. On May 25th the ships reached Dover, and Pepys saw the King being welcomed back to his country by General Monk and by the Mayor of Dover, who gave the King a Bible as his first present on his return to England. The King and his party then set off for London in coaches, with the crowds cheering and shouting all the way.

Pepys had to stay with his cousin on board ship for a while, but soon they were both back in London. Everyone there was trying to get one of the positions at Court or one of the government posts, and the King had a hard task, for he wanted to reward both those who had been loyal to him all the time, and also those supporters of Cromwell who had yet helped in the end to bring him back to his throne. Pepys heard in June that he was one of the lucky ones, as we shall read later.

So Charles was "restored" to the throne. The Restoration was not so fortunate for everyone, however. Pepys wrote in his diary on October 13th, 1660, that he had been to see Major General Harrison hanged: "he looking as cheerful as any man could do in that condition." Harrison had been one of the judges who had condemned Charles I to death, and so he was one of those whom the new king said he could not forgive. "Thus it was my chance", wrote Pepys that night, "to see the King beheaded at White Hall, and to see the first blood shed in revenge for the King at Charing Cross."

In April, 1661, all was ready for the Coronation of the King. Triumphal arches were erected and the streets were decorated; Pepys wrote that it was hardly possible to walk in London, so thick were the crowds who had come to see the decorations. The custom at that time was for the King to spend a night in the Tower of London before his Coronation, and then to go in procession to the Palace, which was in Whitehall, on the day before the ceremony. Pepys and some friends hired a room in Cornhill where they could watch the procession from the Tower in comfort. He wrote that night that the houses and streets were so gaily decorated that they "made brave show", and that the procession was so glorious that "we were not able to look at it, our eyes at last being so much overcome." But really Pepys had seen everything, and he was proud of his cousin's appearance in the procession in a suit so richly embroidered that it had cost £200 even in those days. He was also delighted that the King and the Duke of York had looked up at his window and had noticed his party cheering them.

The picture across the bottom of this page and the next shows you part of the procession as one watcher saw it. Can you see Charles riding on the horse?

The following day, April 23rd, was Coronation Day. Pepys was able to get a seat in Westminster Abbey, but he could not see the ceremony from where he sat, though he could hear the King being proclaimed King Charles II. So he slipped out before the end of the service, and went into Westminster Hall. Here a banquet was to be held after the Coronation ceremony. Scaffolding had been put up round the Hall so that thousands of people could sit there to watch the procession coming in from the Abbey. Pepys met his wife there, and they had a good view of the King as he came in wearing his crown and carrying his sceptre in his hand.

Then Elizabeth and Samuel went home. It had started to rain, so there were not so many fireworks as Pepys had

expected, but he said that there was a glow over the city at night from all the bonfires. In the courtyard outside their own house they found three bonfires and a great party going on. "They laid hold of us and would have us drink the King's health upon our knees, kneeling on a *faggot*, which we all did, they drinking to us one after another."

That night Pepys ended his account of the Coronation Day by writing, "Now, after all this, I can say, that, besides the pleasures of the sight of these glorious things, I may now shut my eyes against any other objects, nor for the future trouble myself to see things of state and show, as being sure never to see the like again in this world." Fortunately for us, Pepys was only saying this after two wonderful days of excitement. He went on "troubling" himself for eight more years with his accounts of all that happened in London.

PEPYS AND THE NAVY

SOON King Charles rewarded Sir Edward Montagu for his services by making him the Earl of Sandwich. Montagu did not forget his young cousin and asked that Pepys should be appointed "Clerk of the Acts". This was the name for the man who was the secretary of the Navy Board, which was that part of the Admiralty that looked after the building, repairing and supplying of the ships for the Navy. The Board had to see that the Royal dockyards were stocked with all the materials needed for shipbuilding and repairing, and that everything needed by the ships at sea was ready for them.

Sir Edward Montagu

14

So the Clerk of the Acts was quite an important man. When his cousin first mentioned it on June 18th, 1660, Pepys could not believe that he would be appointed. On June 23rd Montagu told him that it was to be given to him. "At which I was glad", Pepys wrote, but still did not dare to feel certain of it. It was not until July 9th that he could really trust in his luck. Then he went "to the Navy Office, where in the afternoon we met and sat, and there I began to sign bills in the Office the first time." His salary was a very good one: it was £350 a year, which would be worth ten times more nowadays, and there was a house to go with it. A great change had come over his fortunes since he had begun his diary only seven months before. Then he had been a poor clerk: now he was a Navy official with a good salary. Certainly he would meet many of the great men of his day, and he would often have to go to the Palace of Whitehall to discuss naval matters with the King's brother, the Duke of York, who was the Lord High Admiral. It was more than Pepys had ever dared to hope for, and Elizabeth and he were very excited about it.

He made a list of the names of the ships in the Navy at the time when he became Clerk of the Acts. There were 156 ships—and five more that he said were "not worthy the charge of repair." The pride of the Fleet was the SOVEREIGN OF THE SEAS. She had been built in 1637 with the Ship Money collected by the King's father, Charles I. Improved during the Commonwealth, she was to serve as the model for the capital ships for the next two hundred years. The SOVEREIGN was armed with cannon all along her three decks, which were "flush" (that is, they were level from stem to stern). In addition, she had a fore-castle, quarterdeck and poop, armed with lighter guns. There were many other three-deckers in the Fleet: among

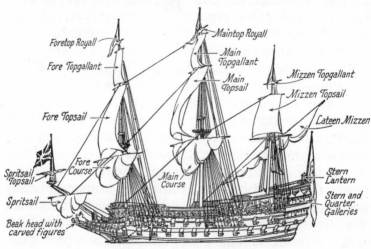

Foretop Royall

Maintop Royall

Fore Topgallant

Main Topgallant

Main Topsail

Mizzen Topgallant

Mizzen Topsail

Fore Topsail

Lateen Mizzen

Spritsail Topsail

Fore Course

Stern Lantern

Spritsail

Main Course

Stern and Quarter Galleries

Beak head with carved figures

The Sovereign of the Seas

them were the ships renamed the PRINCE and the ROYAL CHARLES by the King when they came to bring him back to England from Holland in 1660. There were also some fine two-deckers, and there were very many small ships which did most of the work at sea in the winter when the great ships had to stay in harbour.

All the ships, except the very small ones, had three masts: the fore-mast, the main-mast, and the mizzen-mast which was not quite so tall as the other two. In this period they also had a small mast at the end of their bowsprits called a spritsail topmast. The larger ships carried about 100 guns, and they had the King on horse-back as their figureheads: the others had a lion rampant, looking very fierce. On the sterns of the ships could be seen the Royal Arms, surrounded by the most elaborate carving of 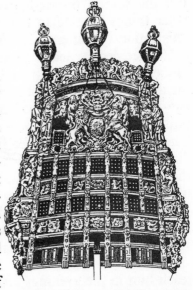 cherubs and bunches of fruit and flowers, all shining with gold paint. You can see from the picture how splendid they must have looked. Even the gunports on the upper and quarterdeck had wreaths of gilded leaves around them.

Pepys knew nothing at all about the Navy when he got his post. Except for the short time he had been with his cousin, he had never been to sea. However, he quickly set to work to learn all he could. An officer, whom he had got to know while he had been on the ROYAL CHARLES, taught him the names of the different parts of a ship. He bought books so that he could learn about work at sea: "Early up in the morning to read 'The Seaman's Grammar and Dictionary' I lately have got, which do please me exceeding well", he wrote on March 13th, 1661. He often went down to the yards to watch the work there: "At five, by water to Woolwich, there to see the manner of tarring, and the several proceedings of making of *cordage*, and other things relating to that sort of works, much to my satisfaction" is an entry on August 8th, 1662.

He decided to learn about the different qualities of timber so that he would understand how to order wood for the Navy. On August 18th, 1662, he went off for the day to the forest at Waltham, where one of the shipbuilders showed him how a surveyor measured timber. They then went on to Ilford for a meal, "and there, while dinner was getting ready, he and I practised measuring of the tables and other things, till I did understand measuring of timber and board very well."

For this work, Pepys found that he needed arithmetic. Although he had been to a very good school and knew Latin and Greek well, he had never learned arithmetic, and he had to ask the mate from the ROYAL CHARLES to teach him in the evenings after he had finished his day's work in the office. He was almost thirty years of age when he began to learn his tables, and for some mornings he got up very early to practise them. "Up by four o'clock, and at my multiplication table hard, which is all the trouble I meet with at all in my arithmetic", he wrote on July 9th, 1662. Two days later he wrote, "Up by four o'clock, and hard at my multiplication table, which I am now almost master of."

But not all this hard work could make his post an easy

one. There was never enough money to do all that should have been done for the Navy. There had been a very good Navy indeed during the Commonwealth, and it had won many fine victories under great admirals like Robert Blake. But this had been done at great expense and the Navy owed a lot of money when the King was restored in 1660. To make matters worse, Parliament did not vote enough money to the King to pay off these debts, let alone to keep up the ships. So from the very first the Navy Board and its secretary had a difficult task. Pepys wrote in his diary on July 31st, 1660, soon after he had been appointed: "to White Hall, where my Lord (his cousin) and the principal officers met, and had a great discourse about raising of money for the Navy, which is in very sad condition, and money must be raised for it. I back to the Admiralty, and there was doing things in order to the calculating of the debts of the Navy and other business, all the afternoon." Some of the ships were sold, but even so Pepys did not know how the Board was going to manage, "since", he wrote on November 10th of that year, "they begin already in Parliament to dispute the paying of the just sea-debts, which were already promised to be paid, and will be the undoing of thousands if they be not paid."

It was partly because the merchants did not know when their bills would be paid that many of them cheated the King in the goods they supplied to the Navy. Pepys felt that he could hardly blame them, but at the same time he did his best to stop them and to see that they sent goods at a fair price and of good quality. Soon after he was appointed, he began to watch the price of ships' stores to see that the King was not being charged too much for his naval supplies. When the ropemaker at the Woolwich yard complained that the merchants were supplying poor hemp to him for the ropes, Pepys went down on June 4th, 1662, to see for himself. He found that "some of it had old stuff that had been tarred, covered over with new hemp, which is such a cheat as has not been heard of. I was glad of this discovery, because I would not have the King's workmen discouraged from representing the faults of merchants' goods, when there is any." Three weeks later, he went "into Thames Street, and there enquire among the ships the price of tar and oil, and do find great content in it, and hope to save the King money by this practice." On another occasion Pepys noticed that the flagmakers were charging eightpence a yard for flags, saying that that was the price in their contract, but when he looked it up, he found that they were charging threepence a yard too much.

Despite all these economies, the Navy Board was always short of money. We get many glimpses in his diary of Pepys' concern over this problem, especially when it meant that he could not pay the sailors their wages. When seamen were discharged at the end of a voyage, they were given tickets which they had to take to the Navy Office to be cashed—and often there was no money there to do so. For example, Pepys wrote on September 28th, 1667, that there would be no money to pay the seamen until January. "Want of money in the Navy puts every thing out of order. Men grow mutinous; and nobody here to mind the business of the Navy but myself," he wrote on October 31st, 1665. And on November 4th of that year he told how he had gone "after dinner, to the office, and much troubled to have 100 seamen all the afternoon there, swearing below, and cursing us, and breaking glass windows, and swear they will pull the house down on Tuesday next. I sent word of this to Court, but nothing will help it but money and a rope."

Worst of all, perhaps, was the plight of prisoners of war, or of the seamen who had been ill or wounded and who wanted to get back to sea again to finish their service. Sailors were signed on for each separate voyage and on a particular ship: if they had been ashore for any reason it was hard to get them to sea again. "The great burden we have upon us at this time at the office", wrote Pepys on September 30th, 1665, "is the providing for prisoners and sick men that are recovered, they lying before our office doors all night and all day, poor wretches. Having been on shore, the Captains won't receive them on board, and other ships we have not to put them in, nor money to pay them off, or provide for them. God remove this difficulty!" In view of all this, and of the dreadful conditions on board the ships, it is not surprising that in time of war the Navy could only get enough men for crews by sending out gangs called *press gangs* to kidnap men and force them on board the ships.

War broke out with the Dutch in 1664. As early as June 28th, 1662, we find Pepys writing, "Great talk there is of fear of a war with the Dutch; and we have order to pitch upon twenty ships to be forthwith set out; but I hope it is but a scare-crow to the world, to let them see that we can be ready for them; though, God knows! the King is not able to set out five ships at this present without great difficulty, we neither having money, credit, nor stores." Yet when war did come, the Navy fought well. A squadron took New Amsterdam from the Dutch and it was renamed New York in honour of the Lord High Admiral, the Duke of York. The Duke himself was with the fleet when it won a victory over the Dutch off Lowestoft in June, 1665, but part of the Navy suffered heavily in a defeat near the mouth of the Thames later.

Here is part of the battle of Lowestoft:

When at sea in battle order, the Fleet sailed in three squadrons—the Red, the White, and the Blue. The Commander-in-Chief was always in the Red squadron which was in the centre; at his maintopmast head he wore either the Royal Standard or the Union flag. The Vice-Admiral of the Fleet carried the Union at the foretopmast head. He was stationed in the White squadron. The Rear-Admiral of the Fleet, who was with the Blue squadron, wore his Union flag at his mizzen. Each squadron wore a suit—ensign, pennant and vane—of a colour matching its name. The Admiral of the White also had a flag of that colour at his main; his Vice at the fore, his rear-admiral white at his mizzen. The flag officers of the Blue were similarly distinguished. Ships, other than the flagships, displayed at maintopmast head

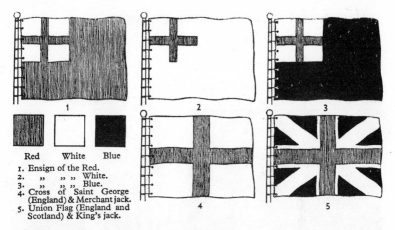

Red   White   Blue

1. Ensign of the Red.
2.   „ „ „ White.
3.   „ „ „ Blue.
4. Cross of Saint George (England) & Merchant jack.
5. Union Flag (England and Scotland) & King's jack.

a pennant with the St. George's cross in miniature at its head. All ships of all the squadrons carried the King's Union Jack at spritsail topmast head. It is from the ensigns of the White squadron that we have the White Ensign for the Royal Navy, while the Red Ensign of the Merchant Navy is derived from the ensigns of the Red squadron.

Pepys visited the Fleet at sea in 1665. He said that it was "a very fine thing to behold, being above 100 ships, great and small: with the flag ships of each squadron distinguished by their several flags on their main, fore or mizzen masts. Among others, the SOVEREIGN, CHARLES, and PRINCE, in the last of which my Lord Sandwich was." Pepys wrote that his cousin received the party kindly when they boarded his ship, but he had a sad account of "the state of the fleet, lacking provisions, having no beer at all, nor have had, most of them, these three weeks or month, and but few days' dry provisions. And indeed he believes that no fleet was ever set to sea in so ill condition of provision, as this was when it went out last."

Here is a scene during a naval battle. Some of the ships are on fire, and many of their sails are shot to pieces:

In 1667, the Government made a great mistake. They thought that the war was as good as over, and in order to save money, part of the fleet was laid up at Chatham. So the Dutch Admiral, De Ruyter, was able to sail up the Thames, destroy the stores at Chatham, and set fire to some of the ships lying in the river there. Pepys wrote in his diary for June 14th, at the time of the Dutch raid, that he had heard that there were Englishmen on board the Dutch ships who cried out to their former shipmates that "We did heretofore fight for tickets, now we fight for dollars." (They meant that it was better to fight for the Dutch and to get their wages paid in Dutch dollars, than to fight for their own country and only get the tickets which often could not be cashed at the Navy Office.) The Dutch captured the ROYAL CHARLES and towed it away with them when they sailed back to Holland.

As a result of this Dutch exploit, the stern of the ROYAL CHARLES is now in a museum in Amsterdam.

In the end, since both the English and the Dutch had their victories and defeats, there was peace in 1667 and England was allowed to keep New York, but Pepys said in his diary that the Dutch had really won the war and "little content most people have in the peace." It was about this time that Pepys felt disheartened about the work he usually enjoyed. He felt that the King was too extravagant and not interested enough in the country, and he wrote that people were beginning to talk with respect about Oliver Cromwell once more.

Nevertheless, both the King and the Duke of York appreciated all the hard work done by Pepys, and told him so many times. On January 28th, 1666, when Pepys had gone to Whitehall to see the Duke of York, "the King come to me of himself, and told me: 'Mr. Pepys' says he 'I do give you thanks for your good service all this year, and I assure you I am very sensible of it'."

When his eyes grew so painful that he could scarcely see to do his work both the King and the Duke of York spoke kindly to Pepys. The Duke arranged for him to have leave of absence from the Navy Office, and then, on May 24th, 1669, took him to see the King who "expressed great sense of my misfortune in my eyes, and concernment for their recovery; and accordingly signified, not only his assent to my desire therein, but commanded me to give them rest this summer."

After his eyesight had improved sufficiently to let him work again, Pepys continued in the Navy Office. King Charles II made him Secretary to the Admiralty in 1673, and the Duke of York relied still more on him when he himself became King James II in 1685. James was unpopular as a king, but he did many fine things for the Navy and he was helped in this work by Pepys. In those later years, however, Pepys had ceased to keep his diary and so we know only from other sources about the improvements which were carried out in the ships and in the conditions for the officers and men. But there is little doubt that, all his life, Pepys felt about his work as he had done one day in 1662 when he wrote in his diary: "My mind is now in a wonderful condition of quiet and content, more than ever in all my life, since my minding the business of my office, which I have done most constantly. My business is a delight to me, and brings me great credit, and," he added quite truthfully, "my purse increases, too."

SAMUEL AND ELIZABETH PEPYS AT HOME

WHEN Pepys began his diary he was living in a very small house in a courtyard called Axe Yard, "having my wife, servant Jane, and no other in the family but us three." Very soon afterwards, however, when he got his new post in the Navy Office, he got a new house with it. Round the Navy Office in Seething Lane there was a courtyard of houses for the main officials of the Board. (Can you find Seething Lane on the map on page 57?) On the very first day that Pepys knew that he was certain to get the post of Clerk of the Acts, he took Elizabeth to see the house they would have. Both of them were delighted with it. Within a week they had moved in, and Pepys wrote in his diary in July 18th, 1660, that he had had his first meal in their new home. Here is the Navy Office, and the courtyard of houses where Samuel and Elizabeth Pepys lived:

When Elizabeth and Samuel first inspected the new house, he asked the Navy Board for permission to make a door leading to a flat roof on a part of the house so that they would be able to walk on it. By August 26th the door had been made, and that night Elizabeth and he strolled on the roof as well as in the garden. Pepys had many other alterations made to the house. Joiners put a new floor in the dining-room, plasterers repaired the ceilings, and glaziers put new panes of glass in the windows. Pepys was so excited about all that was being done to his house that he often went home in the middle of the day just to see how the work was getting on. Sometimes he wrote crossly: "Looking after my workmen whose laziness do much trouble me", but sometimes it was "all the after-noon among my workmen and did give them drink and very merry with them." He hoped to have the workmen out of the house and everything finished in time to have a party at Christmas time, but it cannot have been quite ready for they did not have their party until January 24th, 1661. His father, however, had been to see him before then, and was very proud of his son's house and of all his fine things.

Pepys never described the house in detail, but judging from the rooms he mentioned in his diary from time to time, it must have been a fairly large one of eight or nine rooms. There was a cellar in which he kept the coal and his wines. On the ground floor was the kitchen and a room which Pepys called his 'closet'—we would say his study—where he kept his books and did most of his reading and writing. On the next floor was the dining-room and the sitting-room—he called it the 'parlour'—where his wife usually sat. Above that were at least three bedrooms. Two years after they had moved in, Pepys had the roof taken off the house and another storey added; this was probably to make the attics in which the servants could sleep, for by then he could afford more help in the house for Elizabeth. Of course, the usual awful thing happened while this alteration was being made. When the roof was off, it poured with rain and the water came through and ruined the other ceilings, so Pepys had to get them done again, too.

Since this house was so much bigger than the one they had lived in before, Pepys had to buy a lot of new furniture and furnishings. There was no wallpaper in those days and so the walls of rooms were either covered with wooden panelling or hung with curtains or *tapestries*. The dining-room and the parlour of Pepys' house were panelled, but even so he bought hangings of green *serge* and gilded leather for the dining-room. Later on, in 1669, he bought a mirror for the dining-room and he arranged for an artist to paint on four panels scenes of the four royal palaces: Whitehall, Hampton Court, Greenwich and Windsor.

For the other rooms he had hangings of different materials, and as he grew richer he was able to replace the first hangings he had bought with even better material. On January 26th, 1666, he wrote, "Pleased mightily with what my poor wife has been doing these eight or ten days with her own hands, like a drudge, in fitting the new hangings of our bedchamber of blue, and putting the old red ones into my dressing-room." Two years later he wrote: "My wife is upon hanging the long chamber, where the girl lies, with the sad *stuff* that was in the best chamber in order to the hanging that, with tapestry." (By 'sad' stuff he meant that it was a dull colour.) Two months later he took Elizabeth and the maid to various shops to look at several sets of tapestries. They finally decided on a set with scenes about the Apostles on them. There were three pieces of tapestries in the set and it cost him £83, "and this we think best for us." No wonder that when he called to see an aunt of his later that same day and saw her new hangings, he thought they were "hangings not fit to be seen with mine."

Among the new furniture which he bought when they moved into the house were some dining-room chairs. These were probably in the new style of the time, like this one—tall-backed chairs, much lighter and more elegant than the chairs which had been made before then. These chairs usually had cane backs and seats, but from his diary it seems that Pepys had leather seats in his chairs. Later on he bought a new table for the dining-room, and this, too, was probably in the new style for tables—a gate-legged table quite different from the long refectory tables which had been made until his day.

Pepys does not tell us exactly what he had in the parlour, but he probably had a table and chairs, and some of his musical instruments such as his spinet—which was like a small piano.

This is what the parlour in Pepys' house looked like:

As the years passed and he could afford luxuries, both Elizabeth and he had their portraits painted, she with her little black dog and he with some music in his hand. (Did you notice the music in the portrait on page 2?) Sometimes Pepys was given presents which helped to make their home more comfortable and these, too, he probably put in the parlour. He was very pleased with a fine Turkey carpet which he was given, and he also had some silver candlesticks and snuffers, and some silver flagons and cups which he arranged as ornaments. For New Year's Day in 1669, Pepys bought his wife for the parlour a little walnut cabinet which he thought was "very pretty" and which cost him £11. It was the custom then to give presents on New Year's Day instead of on Christmas Day

There was no new style of beds in the bedrooms, however. Pepys still slept in a four-poster bed which looked very much the same as the beds that people had used since Elizabethan times. There were heavy curtains round the bed: these were drawn at night to shut out the light and the draughts. When Pepys and his wife sent away all their furniture at the time of the Fire of London, he spent one night at the house of a friend who had kept his beds but had sent away his curtains for safety. Pepys said that it was the first time that he had ever slept in a "naked bed" and he felt very strange sleeping in it without any curtains around him. But there was one new idea in bedroom furniture at this time: people began to keep their clothes in sets of drawers instead of in chests, though they still called them "a chest of drawers"—and so do we. Here you can see a chest of drawers of this time, and the sort of bed that Pepys liked to sleep in:

The room Pepys mentioned most in his diary was his closet, for that was his study where he did most of his writing and where he kept his books. He liked to buy books, especially about ships or the Navy, for he loved his work and meant to write a history of the Navy one day. He also bought pictures of ships for the walls of his study. He kept his books in a new sort of bookcase. Instead of keeping them on shelves or in a chest, he bought large cupboards with glass doors. The bookcases which he bought for his books in 1666 are in the library of his College in Cambridge now, and to this day they still have his own books in them.

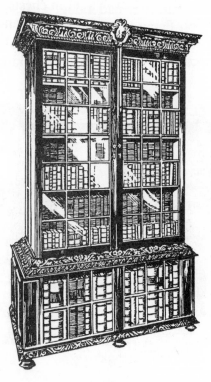

His writing-desk was a small one resting on a table, and there he would sit happily for hours until late at night, reading his books or writing up his diary.

It was not until the end of January, 1661, that the workmen were out of the house. All the alterations which Pepys wanted were not quite finished, and it was to be some years before he had bought all the furniture and hangings that he wanted, but at least the house was neat enough for his wife and him to have in some of their friends to their first party. Everything went off well, except that the chimney smoked.

Elizabeth and Samuel were very happy in the new home. They never had any children, but there was Jane and another servant, and they had a dog, a cat, and two cages of canaries. Soon Pepys was able to afford more servants to help Elizabeth. By 1663 they had three maids and a boy. Here they are cooking dinner at the huge kitchen fire:

If they were having a very important party, they used to get in an extra servant for the day to help with the cooking and to see that the tables were set properly and the napkins folded well. Usually, however, their own servants did all the work. One girl cleaned the rooms, another was the cook with a girl to help her in the kitchen. The boy answered the door, carried the coals from the cellar to the rooms where the fires were wanted, and walked in the streets at night with his master, carrying a lantern to light the way. The boy was dressed in a uniform of grey with black and gold lace, and he wore a sword when they were out at night. Pepys thought that his boy looked smarter than any of his neighbours' boy servants—though he was rather envious of one neighbour who had a black boy called Mingo.

Everyone in the household worked very hard and rose early in the morning. If it was washing day, Elizabeth and the maids would rise at 4 a.m. to start the day's washing, and sometimes they had not finished by the time Pepys went to bed late at night. Whenever they had a party, Elizabeth got up at 5 a.m. to buy specially good food at the market and to have everything ready in time. Pepys, too, used to rise very early—sometimes as early as 4 a.m.—so that he would have time to read or to practise his music before going to the office.

Yet this did not mean that they went to bed early. Pepys often read until after midnight and he once wrote that he had worked until 4 o'clock in the morning, having risen at 5 o'clock on the previous morning. Since all this reading at night had to be done by candle-light, it is not surprising that his eyes gave him trouble. He was always trying to find a way of using candles so that they would give him a better light. Once he bought a globe of glass

with a frame of oiled paper: this, he thought, would make the candle give a good light and take away the glare from his eyes. It probably looked like the one shown here.

Sometimes the Pepys family would have very simple meals. If it was washing day, they just had cold meat for dinner. But when they had friends in for a meal, they would have a great variety of dishes. This is what they had for dinner when they gave a party in 1660 before they moved into the Navy Office house and while they were still quite poor: "A dish of marrow bones; a leg of mutton; a loin of veal; a dish of fowl, three pullets and a dozen of larks all in a dish; a great tart; a neat's tongue (ox tongue); a dish of anchovies; a dish of prawns and cheese." Pepys was fond of strongly flavoured food: perhaps to our taste the strangest thing is the sort of breakfast he would have. This is what he had one morning for breakfast: oysters, neat's tongue, anchovies, wine and ale.

In 1663 the Pepys had a party for some important friends. Samuel was anxious to impress them. It was one of the times when they got an extra cook in for the day. Pepys was worried in case the jack—the rod in front of the open fire in the kitchen on which the meat was roasted—would not turn well so that the meat would not get thoroughly cooked; but it did. They began that meal with oysters, then they had a hash of rabbit and lamb, then a great joint of beef. After that they had a dish of roasted fowl, and ended with a tart and fruit and cheese. Pepys felt that "my dinner was noble and enough." They had fires in all the rooms that night. Pepys was delighted to find that the new table in his dining-room could take eight people quite comfortably, and he thought that it could take nine or ten people if need be. Before his guests left in the evening, they were given some cold meat and some sack posset—a drink of wine and hot milk— and they left at 10 o'clock "both them and myself highly pleased with our arrangements this day." He thought that the whole day would cost him about £5, but Elizabeth had enough food left over to be able to offer cold meat to visitors for the next few days.

Whenever friends came to see him or to have a meal with him, Pepys loved to show them over the house and to let them see the latest books or pictures or pieces of furniture which he had bought. He was very proud of his house and of all the lovely things he had in it. When he began his diary in 1660 he was living in a small house and was quite poor: by the time he had to stop writing his diary in 1669, he had a lovely home furnished at great cost and with much care.

THE CLOTHES PEPYS AND HIS WIFE WORE

WHEN we first meet Pepys on January 1st, 1660, he was wearing "my suit with great skirts, having not lately worn any other clothes but them." This was a black suit, but he also had a good white suit trimmed with silver lace which he wore on February 2nd. Men at this time wore a long coat with full skirts almost down to their knees, very wide breeches bound round the knees with ribbon or lace, thread or silk stockings, and shoes tied with laces. They wore their hair long and curled on their shoulders, and they had very wide brimmed hats.

With the return of the King, clothes became much gayer in colour than they had been under the Commonwealth, but the style did not change very much. Pepys wrote on July 1st, 1660, that he, too, had been getting some smarter clothes: "this morning come home my fine camlet cloak with gold buttons, and a silk suit, which cost me much money, and I pray God to make me able to pay for it." (Camlet was a woven material that in Pepys' days was made from goat's hair.) This was the first time that Pepys had been able to afford suits made of silk. In October, Pepys noticed that the fashionable men were wearing cloaks shorter than before, so he got his father, who was a tailor, to change his long black cloak for a short one—"long cloaks being now quite out."

As Pepys grew prosperous, he decided that he ought to dress better and that he could afford to wear the very latest fashion. In 1662 men began to wear buckled shoes,

Old Style

and so Pepys got buckles for his shoes. In October, 1663, he decided to have some new suits and a cloak, and he asked his wife and his brother to go with him to choose the material. He got a cloak made of cloth but lined with velvet, a black waistcoat, two black shirts, a purple velvet suit trimmed with black buttons, and there was enough velvet left to make him a hat to match. Although Pepys had some light-coloured suits, he usually wore black suits with red ribbons or blue stockings to brighten them up.

In 1663 he had a wig made, for it had become fashionable for men to wear wigs instead of their own hair. He was delighted when he heard that the King and the Duke of York were also having wigs made. Pepys tried on his

39

The Duke of York, who became King James II

wig as soon as it arrived, and he liked himself in it so much that he had his hair cut off, and he asked the wigmaker to make another wig for him out of his own hair. His maids all came in to see him in the new wig: they liked him in it but they were sorry that he had had his hair cut short. Then Pepys went for a walk to show off his own wig. He went to the office in it the next morning and was quite disappointed because "no great matter made of my periwig as I was afraid there would be." By the Sunday he was still feeling rather strange in his wig when he went to church "where I found that my coming in a periwig did not prove so strange as I was afraid it would, for I thought that all the church would presently have cast their eyes all upon me, but I found no such thing." Perhaps after all that, it was a great relief to Pepys that the Duke of York noticed the periwig. For, when he went the next day to discuss naval matters, the Duke teased him and said that "Mr. Pepys was so altered with his new periwig that he did not know him."

In those days people did not worry about cleanliness and did not often have baths. Elizabeth sometimes went to the public bathhouse but Pepys only mentions bathing his feet. Wigs in particular were difficult to keep clean. Pepys used to get one of the maids to comb his hair and his wigs—and sometimes she found lice in both. In the end he found it easier to pay his barber twenty shillings a year to keep his wigs clean and in good order. The barber would re-pair the wigs if they needed it. Once Pepys was sealing a letter and he must have put his head too near the candle, for he heard the crackling of hair just in time to warn him before the wig caught fire.

New Style

In 1666 the style of men's clothes changed a great deal. The King announced on October 8th that he was going to set a new fashion and to wear plainer clothes to try to teach the nobles not to spend so much money on their dress. On October 13th Pepys saw the King and the Duke of York trying on the new style of coat, and on October 15th the King wore his in public for the first time. Pepys said that it was "a long *cassock* close to the body, of black cloth, and pinked with white silk under it, and a coat over it, and the legs ruffled with black ribbons like a pigeon's leg: and, upon the whole, I wish the King may keep it, for it is a very fine and handsome garment." (Pinked means that there were holes or cuts in the black cloth so that the white silk underneath could be seen.) Needless to say, Pepys was not happy until he, too, had a new suit made for him, like the King's. He wrote on November 4th, that "my tailor's man brings

my *vest* home, and coat to wear with it, and belt and silver-hilted sword: so I rose and dressed myself, and I like myself mightily in it, and so does my wife."

Fashions for men altered much more than fashions for women in the years when Pepys was writing. The skirts of the women's dresses were full and were usually gathered up to show a petticoat underneath, and both were trimmed with lace. The picture shows you the kind of dress Elizabeth would have worn. Elizabeth, like Samuel, wore a lot of black, but she also wore blue and green a great deal. Pepys liked to see her well dressed.

He wrote, for example, on June 29th, 1662: "To church with my wife, who this day put on her green petticoat of flowered satin, with fine white and black lace of her own putting on, which is very pretty." He liked a blue dress that she wore once when friends came to dinner, and she had a flowered taffeta frock which she had on one night when they went to the theatre "and everyone in love with it." She had, however, a blue dress with a white satin bodice: Samuel did not like this dress at all, and he was cross when she wore it. Women rarely wore hats, but when they did, they wore large flat hats like a man's. Pepys once saw one of the great ladies of the court wearing a large hat with a red feather in it. About 1665, however, women began to wear hoods over their heads when they went out of doors. When Elizabeth went to church on Whit-Sunday in 1665, she wore a new yellow hood.

Women wore shoes which were almost like slippers, made of coloured brocades or silk. That meant that when they went out in the streets, they had to wear something over their shoes to protect them from the dirt. These overshoes were called pattens. They had wooden soles, to raise the wearer an inch or two from the ground, and there were leather straps to fasten the pattens on to the shoes They were not very comfortable, but at least they kept the pretty shoes clean and dry. Elizabeth often had bother with her pattens. Once, when they were going to church, her husband got very impatient with her because she walked so slowly and could not keep up with him. On another occasion, Pepys was walking with Lady Batten, a neighbour, and one of her pattens got stuck in the mud so that she had to leave it behind her in the street "at which she was horribly vexed and I led her, vexing her a little more in mirth." Later, pattens were made specially for each pair of shoes, so they fitted better.

Here are different sorts of shoes and pattens:

Women were not, in fact, at all well clad for bad weather. Their shoes were hardly suitable, they rarely wore hats except when riding, and they do not seem to have had warm cloaks to wear over their dresses. More often they just had little capes called whisks. In the cold weather in November 1660, Pepys and his wife went shopping and "she bought her a white whisk and put it on, and I a pair of gloves." When it was very cold, both men and women wore muffs. On November 30th, 1662, Pepys wrote: "This day I first did wear a muff, being my wife's last year's muff; and now I have bought her a new one, this serves me very well."

Women began to copy the men's fashion of wearing wigs, but the fashion did not catch on at this time. Most women wore their hair in ringlets and curls. Certainly Pepys did not like it when Elizabeth tried to wear a wig, partly because she wanted to wear a fair wig when her own hair was dark. "This day", he wrote on March 13th, 1665, "my wife began to wear light coloured locks, quite white almost, which, though it makes her look very pretty, yet, not being natural, vexes me, that I will not

44

have her wear them." A fashion he did like, however, was that of wearing little black patches on the face. Elizabeth began to wear them in 1660 and he thought they made her look very pretty. Once he was at the theatre and he saw one of the great ladies of the Court sending for her maid and putting a patch on her face; he wondered if it was because she felt a pimple coming up.

Elizabeth was very fond of jewellery, especially of pearls, and Pepys gave her several strings as presents at different times. Once she saw a ring of turquoise set with little diamonds which she asked him to give her for her St. Valentine's Day present. At the time, Pepys was feeling rather guilty about the amount of money he spent on himself in going to the theatre so much, and he felt that she cost him little "compared with other wives and I have not many occasions to spend money on her." So Elizabeth got her ring! It was the custom then for men and women to give each other presents on St. Valentine's Day, but a pair of embroidered gloves, like these, or a pair of stockings was more usual.

Pepys and his wife took great care of their clothes because they cost so much. Sometimes, in fact, Pepys changed his clothes during the day because he would not risk his good clothes if he thought the weather might spoil them. For example, on May 1st, 1669, he wrote:

"First put on a summer suit this year; but it was not my fine one of flowered *tabby* vest, and coloured camlet tunic, because it was too fine with the gold lace at the bands, that I was afraid to be seen in it; but put on the *stuff* suit I made the last year, which is now repaired; and so did go to the Office in it, and sat all the morning, the day looking as if it would be foul. At noon home to dinner, and there find my wife extraordinarily fine, with her fine flowered tabby gown that she made two years ago, now laced exceedingly pretty; and, indeed, was fine all over; and mighty earnest to go, though the day was very lowering; and she would have me put on my fine suit, which I did."

It is not surprising that Pepys was so careful. He paid £24 for his suits—and we have to remember that that means perhaps ten times as much nowadays. Elizabeth made many of her own clothes, but the cost of the petticoat alone would be £5 by the time she had paid twenty-six shillings a yard for the material and had the lace to buy as well. Fortunately, since both men and women's clothes were so gay, material from either of their clothes could be used to mend or alter the other's. The gold lace from Elizabeth's wedding dress was used to edge a coat for her husband once the gown was finished, and Pepys had a grey suit which had white facings made from one of Elizabeth's petticoats.

Then, too, they both had loose gowns which they wore in the house to save their good clothes. Pepys said of Elizabeth's housegown that "I used to call it her kingdom from the ease and comfort she had in the wearing of it." He called the loose gown which men wore a "night gown", but by that he meant what we would call a dressing-gown.

46

Pepys felt that money on clothes was well spent. He liked new clothes, and he liked to make a good impression on other people by looking so well dressed and prosperous. He liked Elizabeth, too, to look well. Once he took her to Court to see the Queen Mother and the two Princesses who were the King's sisters. He was very proud indeed when he looked at Princess Henrietta, the King's favourite sister, and felt that "my wife standing near her with two or three black patches on, and well dressed, did seem to me much handsomer than she."

Elizabeth Pepys

TWO THINGS PEPYS LIKED TO DO

PEPYS often mentioned in his diary the things he did in his spare time when his work in the Office was finished. He belonged to the Royal Society, which had just been founded for men interested in science, and Pepys used to go to some of its meetings to see experiments. He liked to go to taverns and coffee-houses to gossip to people. But what he liked to do more than anything else was to go to the theatre, or else to take part in some music, either by singing or by playing one of his many instruments.

He went to the theatre a great deal, sometimes as often as six times in one week. Once he saw thirty plays in three months. He was always making good resolutions not to go to the theatre so much—but he usually ended by breaking them. The two important theatres at the time Pepys was writing his diary were the Theatre Royal in Drury Lane, which Pepys called the 'King's Playhouse', and the Duke of York's Theatre in Lincoln's Inn Fields, which Pepys called the 'Duke's Playhouse'. There were also a few small and less fashionable theatres known as 'nurseries' because actors trained in them, and then the best would go on to one of the two big theatre companies. Pepys went to these small theatres, too, but usually he preferred to go to the 'King's Playhouse' and the 'Duke's Playhouse'. The actors there were treated as though they were the servants of the King or the Duke. The actors at the Theatre Royal, for example, wore a scarlet uniform to show that they were royal servants. Opposite you can see the stage of the Duke of York's Theatre. Notice especially the coat of arms and elaborate design above it.

48

Neither of these two theatre buildings remain today, so
we do not know exactly what they looked like. (There is
still a Theatre Royal in Drury Lane, but the building is a
much later one.) We do know, however, a little of what
they must have looked like from some drawings and from
Pepys' descriptions of his many visits to the theatres. It
seems that they had changed a good deal from the

theatres of Shakespeare's time and that they were beginning to look more like our own. They had a stage not unlike ours, though there was still a part which jutted out in front into the audience on which the actors usually acted, leaving the part where our actors now perform for scenery. Scenery was being used for the first time and it was often very elaborate. The orchestra sometimes sat below the stage, where it is now, instead of on the stage or in a gallery above it—but Pepys did not like it there. Also for the first time, women's parts were taken by actresses instead of being played by boys.

For the audience, there was the pit where spectators could stand or sit on benches, then a circle of boxes, and then there was a gallery. One theatre, at least, must have had a second row of boxes near the stage, for Pepys once took an 'upper box'. Pepys often went to the pit, but he preferred to be in a box so that he could be near the fashionable people from the Court and watch them as well as the play. Although there was a small theatre at Whitehall for private performances at Court, both the King and the Duke often went to the public theatres. If they, or members of the Court, were not there when Pepys went to the theatre, he was quite disappointed: "not so well pleased with the company today, which was full of citizens —there hardly being a gallant man or woman in the house."

Pepys tells us that he paid half a crown to go into the pit, but that it cost twenty shillings if he took a box. There were cheaper seats in the gallery at a shilling and eighteen pence, and that was what he paid in his younger, poorer days. He often bought oranges when he went to the theatre, and they cost sixpence each.

There was one rather strange thing allowed then. You

could go into the pit to look at a play for a short while without paying: if you stayed for more than one act, the doorman came to collect the money from you, but if you did not like the play and decided not to stay, then you could just walk out without paying. Pepys had done this one night when he wrote in his diary: "To the Nursery, but the house did not act today: and so I to the other two playhouses into the pit, to gaze up and down, and there did by this means, for nothing, see an act in 'The School of Compliments' at the Duke of York's house, and then 'Henry the Fourth' at the King's house; but not liking either of the plays, I took my coach again, and home."

Pepys had very decided views about the plays he saw. He did not like 'A Midsummer Night's Dream' at all, "which I have never seen before nor shall again, for it is the most ridiculous play that I ever saw in my life." He saw other plays by Shakespeare that he liked very much— for example, 'Macbeth', 'Hamlet', and 'The Tempest'. He liked many plays so much that he went to see them over and over again, but many of them were plays that are never acted today. Sometimes he saw a puppet play: once he heard that a puppet show that he had enjoyed had been taken to Whitehall for a performance before the King.

It was a very sad day for Pepys when he began to find that he could no longer enjoy visits to the theatre. Hundreds of candles were needed to light the stage, and they dazzled his eyes. As his eyesight grew weaker he had to stop going to the theatre so much—but sometimes he went just the same.

Besides going to the theatre as often as he could, Pepys had a great love of music. He often mentions singing or playing a musical instrument, and he enjoyed a play still more if it had some music or songs in it.

He seems to have been able to play quite a number of instruments himself. When he was young, his father had taught him to play the viol, which was an early form of the violin. He himself, however, preferred a flageolet, which was a wind instrument with a mouthpiece, six holes and keys, rather like our flute. (You can see a viol on the left and a flageolet on the right.) He usually had a flageolet in his pocket wherever he went; he would play it in a coach to pass the time on a journey, and he would practice on it while walking in the park or out on the roof of his house. Once, when he was being shown over a large house, he noticed that there was an "excellent echo" in the cellar, so he took out his flageolet and played it there. He was delighted when the man who made his pipes for him showed him a way of "having two pipes of the same note fastened together, so that I can play on one and then echo it on the other, which is mighty pretty." He also liked to play the theorbo, which was a kind of lute; it was played by plucking the strings with the right hand while using the left hand for the finger-board, rather as we play a banjo. He played a recorder well, too, and took great pains to get the right fingering for it.

The only instrument he did not like was the guitar, even though he was given the King's guitar to look after on the voyage back to England in 1660. The guitar, however, was a very popular instrument at that time. There was a sort of guitar called a cittern, which most barbers kept in their shops so that customers could amuse themselves by playing on it while waiting their turn to be shaved. It must often have been noisy in barbers' shops, for after Charles II had landed at Dover in 1660, those left on board ship had a concert with the instruments they had with them and using "two candlesticks with money in them" for cymbals: Pepys said that the noise they made with their little home-made orchestra was like "barber's music." Here you can see a cittern.

His great love of music was shared by many others in England in his day. Pepys often mentioned that he had visited friends for dinner and that afterwards they had all played together on their viols and lutes. Here is a group of friends enjoying a musical evening:

At taverns, groups of men would join to sing songs or to play their instruments. Pepys tells us, for example, of a visit to a coffee-house on February 21st, 1660, when he and his friends ended by singing "a variety of brave Italian and Spanish songs." Once he had to share a boat on the river with a stranger "and he proved a man of love to music, and he and I sang together all the way down with great pleasure." When families were trying to save their most precious belongings from the Great Fire of 1666, Pepys noticed that "hardly one lighter or boat in three that had the goods of a house in, but there was a pair of virginals in it", so there must have been many homes in London with virginals. Pepys himself had a spinet and a harpsichord as well as a virginal in his own home. (These were all early forms of the piano, with a keyboard, but the strings were plucked, whereas in a piano the strings are hit by hammers.)

Spinet

Virginal

Pepys took singing lessons and practised in the mornings before he went to work, and he had Elizabeth taught to sing, too. He tried to choose servants who had good voices so that his little household would be able to sing part songs together. "After dinner", he wrote one night, "my wife and Mercer, and Tom and I, sat till eleven at night, singing and fiddling, and a great joy it is to see me master of so much pleasure in my own house that it is and will be still I hope a great pleasure for me to be at home. The girl plays pretty well upon the harpsichord, but only ordinary tunes, but hath a good hand; sings a little but hath a good voice and ear. My boy, a brave boy, sings finely." Another night "we stayed singing in the garden until supper was ready and there was great pleasure."

We still sing today some of the songs he mentions. He liked 'Greensleeves'. When he was on board the NASEBY going to meet the King, they made up new words to the tune of 'Greensleeves' to make fun of the 'Rump' —that was the nickname for the old Parliament of the Commonwealth. Another song he was fond of was the Scottish one called 'Barbara Allan'.

He was not content, however, just to play and sing other people's songs. He loved to compose for himself, and he had a music master for a while to teach him to write down music and to help him with the setting of his own compositions. It gave him great pleasure to hear his own songs sung by his friends. There was one song in particular he was very proud of: it was called 'Beauty Retire', and he held the music for it in his hand when he had his portrait painted.

Elizabeth did not have the same delight in music as her husband, and she must sometimes have had a rather hard time with him. Once Samuel wrote: "Some time I spent this morning beginning to teach my wife some scale in music and found her apt beyond imagination." But more often his entries in his diary were more like this one: "Before dinner making my wife to sing. Poor wretch! her ear is so bad that it made me angry, till the poor wretch cried to see me so vexed at her, till I think I shall not discourage her again." Later on he found a friend so poor at music that she was "worse than my wife a thousand time, so it doth a little reconcile me to her." When Pepys was sorry, as he often was, that he had been so busy with work at the Office that he had not had time to play any of his instruments, perhaps Elizabeth was glad.

One night Elizabeth and he had a quarrel about his music. That night Pepys wrote in his diary something that we can see was true throughout his whole life: "Music is the thing of all the world that I love best."

THE LONDON IN WHICH PEPYS LIVED

THE LONDON in which Pepys lived was a busy crowded city. It was much the largest town in England, but it was still a very small place compared with the London that we know today. It was, in fact, little more than that part we call the City of London: that is, roughly, the part of London which lies between the Tower of London and St. Paul's Cathedral. Here is a plan showing London in the time of Pepys.

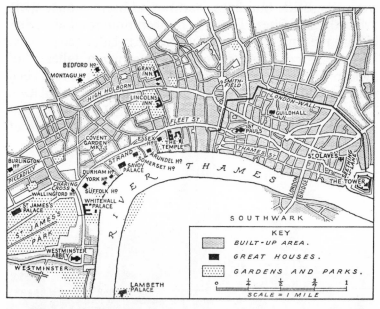

Pepys' London had not changed much since medieval and Elizabethan days. It was still entered by gates through the high medieval city walls: names like Ludgate, Cripplegate and Moorgate tell us where the gateways were. The King lived at Whitehall, and the city of

Westminster was linked with London by a line of fairly recent houses. Most of the places which we now think of as part of London were then villages well away in the country. There were villages like Kensington where Pepys and his wife would go in the evenings for some fresh air, or Islington where they would eat the famous cheesecakes made there, or Rotherhithe where they went to pick cowslips in the spring.

Inside the city walls, where Pepys lived, London was a tightly packed town of crowded streets. There were very few brick buildings, and not many of stone, apart from the churches. There were over a hundred churches within the small city. St. Paul's Cathedral was the greatest and largest of them all. It had been even taller until Queen Elizabeth's reign, when the high steeple had been knocked down by lightning in 1561 and never replaced, so that only a tall square tower was left. Here is the great Cathedral towering above the houses and churches of the City:

The Cathedral and the churches were in the Gothic style of architecture, with slender columns and lofty pointed arches. Only a few of the churches escaped the Fire of London in 1666. One of them is the church to which Pepys went most often: the Church of St. Olave's in Hart Street, just at the top of the lane in which he lived. This is what St. Olave's looked like when Pepys worshipped there:

Pepys usually mentioned on a Sunday where he had been to church that day, what he thought of the sermon, and who had been in church. He had gone to St. Olave's when he wrote on June 18th, 1665: "Up, and to church, where Sir W. Pen was the first time since he came from sea, after the battle. Mr. Mills made a sorry sermon." But he also liked to try all the other churches, too, as he had done on the Sunday on which he wrote: "This morning, till churches were done, I spent going from one church to another, and hearing a bit here and there."

St. Olave's has been repaired many times, but below you can still see in it the style of a church built in the fifteenth century. Elizabeth Pepys' monument is on the wall.

Most of the houses in London were made of wood. The better houses had brick or stone foundations, and the walls were made by filling in a wooden frame with laths and covering those with plaster. Each storey of the house projected out above the lower one, until the top storey overhung the street so much that it almost met the top storey of the house opposite. The roofs were usually covered with red tiles. The houses of the poorer people were smaller and made entirely of wood, with roofs of wood covered with tar. They were all built so close together that they could catch fire easily.

There were a few wide streets, like Cheapside, but most of the streets were dark and airless because of the overhanging houses. They were cobbled and had no pavements, but there was a gutter down the middle. People threw their rubbish into the streets, and it collected in the gutters until men came with carts to carry it away outside the city walls. This street, which you can still see today in York, shows how most of London's streets would have looked at this time:

There was no sanitation or drainage at all in London then, and so the streets must have been filthy to walk in, and very smelly, especially in the hot weather. There was, however, a water supply, though the water was not very pure. For most of the city, the water was brought from the river Lea by the New River and then by wooden pipes to fountains in some of the main streets. For the lower part of the town, the water was pumped up from the Thames by a water-wheel at London Bridge. Because of the poor sanitary conditions, there were many bad epidemics before the terrible plague of 1665 in which so many Londoners died.

There were often traffic jams in the narrow streets. Coaches and waggons bringing goods in from the country would block the streets so that no one could pass. Those who had not coaches of their own could hire a small coach, just as we might hire a taxi, to go short distances in the city. These were called hackney coaches. In order to keep the streets clear of waiting traffic, the King forbade hackney coaches to stand in the streets, but Pepys wrote on November 7th, 1660, that "notwithstanding this was the first day of the King's proclamation against hackney coaches coming into the streets to stand to be hired, yet I got one to carry me home."

This is the sort of coach that Pepys saw in the streets:

Even those streets wide enough to let coaches pass easily were made difficult for traffic by lines of stalls down the middle. This often led to accidents. Once Pepys was in a hackney coach when it was stopped by some butchers who said that the coach had knocked into their stall and damaged their meat. "They said that the coachman had done 40s. or £5 of harm: but going down I saw that he had done little or none: and so I gave them a shilling for it and they were well contented."

About the time Pepys was keeping his diary, coaches began to have glass in their windows. Before then there had only been leather curtains to draw across the open window frames or door if the weather was cold or windy. Pepys was not sure whether the glass windows were an improvement or not. Once he was in a hackney coach which could not get up a narrow lane near St. Paul's Cathedral because of other coaches and carts, so his driver tried to turn back. In doing this, he overturned the coach into a cellar. Pepys and the friend who was with him were able to jump clear because it was one of the older coaches with open sides, but he wondered afterwards if they would have been able to escape if they had been in a 'glass coach' as he called it.

For longer journeys to other parts of England, there were much bigger coaches, drawn by perhaps six or eight horses, which set out from some of the yards of the big inns in the city. Some of Pepys' relations lived in Cambridgeshire, so when any of his family who lived in London wanted to visit them, they went to the George Inn in Holborn where they could get a coach to Cambridge. There were also waggons which carried both passengers and goods. At the time of the plague in 1665, Pepys' mother left it too late to get a seat in the coach to

Cambridge and she had to travel there in the waggon. If Pepys was going on a journey by himself he did not usually go by coach, but hired a horse to ride. Here is a waggon for carrying heavy goods:

By 1668 Pepys felt rich enough to be able to afford to buy a coach of his own instead of spending so much money on hiring hackney coaches. He asked the advice of several of his friends before he decided on a light one which would take four people and was drawn by a pair of horses. He was a very proud man the first time that he and his wife were able to come home from the theatre in their own coach instead of having to hire a hackney coach. In the spring of the next year, Pepys had the coach painted silver, and then varnished yellow; he dressed his coachman in green and red; he had green reins, and the tails of the horses were tied up with red ribbon; and then he and his wife went for a drive in Hyde Park in their newly-painted coach on May Day. Everything looked so smart that he thought "people did mightily look upon us; and the truth is, I did not see any coach more pretty."

Pepys, like most other Londoners in those days, used the river a great deal as a means of travelling. Very often it was quicker and safer to go from one part of London to another by boat than to try to walk or drive through the streets. There were steps down to the water at many places along the Thames, and boats were always waiting there to be hired, though sometimes Pepys had to share one with another passenger if the boatman was busy. This was the way he usually went up to Whitehall to see the Duke of York, and he often went down by boat to Deptford or to Woolwich to visit the ship-yards there or to inspect the ships.

Here is the Palace of Whitehall seen from the river where many small boats are taking people up and down stream:

At night the streets were dark and very dangerous. Everyone whose house faced on to the street had to put a candle in a lantern and hang it outside his house "from such time as it grows dark until nine o'clock in the evening." After that, there was no street lighting at all. If people had to be out after 9 o'clock, they would hire boys who stood at the street corners and carried torches to light the travellers home. These were called link-boys. Sometimes the link-boys had other uses besides lighting

Londoners home through the dark streets. Pepys told of one boy who rushed into a house one night to tell the family that their house was falling down. The family was playing cards and they thought that the boy said that their house was on fire, but thanks to his warning, they all got out in time before the house collapsed.

If it was dark before Pepys left the house, he used to get his maid to go with him to carry a lantern to show him the way, and then he would hire a link-boy to bring him back home. Later on, when he could afford a boy as a servant, it was one of the boy's duties to light his master through the streets at night. Once, when Pepys was coming home from the theatre, the coach he had hired stuck on a hill because the horses were tired, so Pepys got out and sent his own boy for a link-boy to stay with them in the dark street until they could find another coach.

In order to protect people and their houses from robbers at night, there were constables for each parish who went round the streets at night to see that everything was safe. We are usually told that these men were not very good or efficient, but Pepys mentions several times when they did good work. Once he could not find a coach to take him over London Bridge in the dark, so he crossed on foot and would have fallen into a hole in the bridge if a constable had not been standing there to warn people, and he caught hold of Pepys in time to save him from breaking his leg. Then there was the time when Pepys and his wife were knocked up in the middle of the night because the constables for their district had found their yard door open and thought there might have been a burglary. But it was simply that the servants had forgotten to lock the door "and so", wrote Pepys, "I desired them to shut the door and bade them goodnight."

A bellman also went round the streets through the night to see that all was well, calling out the time and the state of the weather as he went his way. "Past one of the clock and a cold, frosty, windy, morning" was called out by the bellman as Pepys sat up late one night writing his diary for the previous day.

There were many shops in London. Usually the bottom room of the house was the shop or office, and the merchant or shopkeeper and his family lived in the rooms upstairs. Here is a typical row of houses and shops in a busy street:

There were also the rows of stalls down the wider streets, and there were many stalls under cover in the Royal Exchange and in Westminster Hall, so that those two places must have looked like covered markets. Pepys bought a lot of his clothes, particularly his shirts, at the stalls in Westminster Hall. Some of the shops sold ready cooked food, which Pepys and his wife sometimes bought and brought home to eat if Elizabeth was ill or too busy to cook.

Pepys mentions so many inns and taverns in his diary that there must have been hundreds of them in London. One of his favourite places was the Dolphin Tavern, near his home. It was one that many naval men went to, and so Pepys got a great deal of news about ships there. People used to meet in taverns to do their business. Once the Pepys family had a quarrel about money and all the relations met in the Pope's Head Tavern to settle it. Pepys often mentioned in his diary what he had had to eat in a tavern that day. Sometimes it was just a quick meal of bread and cheese and ale, but sometimes in the evenings he would have a big meal there and then he and his friends would settle down for a night of singing and playing their instruments in the tavern. Poor Elizabeth must often have been left alone in the evening.

There was only one newspaper allowed at the time, 'The London Gazette'. It was rather dull and had not much news in it. So men liked to meet in the taverns to talk to each other and to hear the news. But in the years when Pepys was writing his diary, a new kind of meeting place became popular. This was the coffee-house, where men met, just as in the taverns, to talk to each other over a cup of coffee. Pepys often went to the coffee-houses, especially to one near Westminster which was a good place in which to hear the gossip about what was happening in Parliament. Coffee was quite a new drink in England —but there were still more new drinks in those years, and of course, Pepys enjoyed trying them and writing about them in his diary. On September 25th, 1660, he wrote: "I did send for a cup of tea (a China drink) of which I never had drunk before." Then on November 24th, 1664, he was in a coffee-house and had something else he had never drunk before—a cup of chocolate. He spelt it "Jocolatte" in his diary that night and said that it was "very good". On the whole, however, Pepys preferred to drink wine, whether in taverns or at home. It was probably just as well that the men and women of Pepys' time usually drank ale or wine, for it must have been much safer to drink than the water.

There were many sights in the streets to interest Londoners. There was the Lord Mayor's Show every November when the Lord Mayor went in procession through the City, much as he does now. Then there was St. Bartholomew's Fair every September. Pepys always enjoyed seeing some of the circus turns in this Fair— the men walking the tight-rope or the horse that could count by pawing on the ground. Each May Day there was dancing in the streets: Pepys described one year how he had met "many milkmaids, with their garlands on their pails, dancing with a fiddler before them."

So, despite all the noise and the bustle and the dangers, Pepys loved living in London. He liked his work, he got a great deal of pleasure from his possessions, and a day rarely passed in which he could not write of a pleasant evening spent entertaining friends at home, or meeting them in a tavern or coffee-house, or going to the theatre, or of something interesting which had taken place in London that day.

THE PLAGUE

ON JUNE 7th, 1665, Pepys noted in his diary that it was the hottest day that he had ever known. His wife and his mother and their maids went off for a day on the river, while he himself met some friends and they dined in the Dolphin Tavern and then went on to Vauxhall Gardens for a walk. As they went through the city, Pepys saw two or three houses in Drury Lane with a red cross and 'Lord have mercy on us' written on their doors. He wrote that night that this was "a sad sight to me, being the first of that kind that, to my remembrance, I ever saw." He knew that it meant that the plague had broken out in those houses, and he bought some roll tobacco to smell and to chew, for he thought this would act as a disinfectant.

The plague was a disease we no longer have in this country. It was a very dangerous fever, probably carried by the black rats which infested the old houses. Few people recovered from it. Though Pepys had never seen the plague sign on doors before, there had often been outbreaks of plague in London: the narrow airless streets and the bad sanitation and drainage made it easy for infectious diseases to spread among the people. Once the plague had started, no-one knew how to treat it. The only thing they could do was to try to stop the disease from spreading. They did this by forbidding anyone from entering or leaving a house where the plague had struck. To show that someone in a house had the plague and that no one should go near it, a red cross was painted and 'Lord have mercy on us' was written on the door. The people in the locked house would call from an upper window if they needed food, and it would be flung up to them.

For the next few days, Pepys did not seem to notice anything more about the plague: he was excited about the good news of an English victory at sea over the Dutch. A few days later, however, he heard that one of his own friends had caught the plague, "but he hath, I hear, gained great goodwill among his neighbours: for he discovered it himself first, and caused himself to be shut up of his own accord: which was very handsome." By the end of that week Pepys wrote, "the town grows very sickly, and people to be afraid of it: there dying this last week of the plague 112, from 43 the week before."

By June 21st, many were beginning to leave London for fear of catching the plague as it grew steadily worse, "the coaches and waggons being all full of people going into the country", as Pepys wrote. He persuaded his wife and his mother to go away, but he himself stayed on.

Here are the people fleeing from London at the time of an earlier plague, in 1630. The plague is shown as a skeleton, with spear raised high, ready to strike:

Pepys went about his usual business discussing plans for the Navy at Court, working hard in his office, but noticing each day as he went about that more and more houses were boarded up because the families in them had caught the plague.

When he went up to Whitehall on June 29th, he found the Palace surrounded by waggons, for it had now been decided to move the Court to Hampton Court for safety. That week 267 people had died of the plague, "the season growing so sickly", wrote Pepys, "that it is much to be feared how a man can escape having a share with others in it, for which the good Lord God bless me! or make me fitted to receive it."

Next week the streets were quieter still, for few were brave enough to stay on to work as he did, and he heard the bells tolling all day long for the dead. He went to a wedding in Greenwich, where he found everyone "afraid of London" so that he had to pretend that he had not come from there. When he visited other friends he realized from what they said that "it is an unpleasant thing to be at Court, everybody being fearful one of another, and all so sad enquiring after the plague." Staying at home to work all one Sunday he wrote, " it was a sad noise to hear our bell to toll and ring so often today, either for deaths or burials; I think, five or six times." On August 10th, he noted that 3,000 people had died of the plague that week, and so he made his will, "the town growing so unhealthy, that a man cannot depend upon living two days."

At first, it had been ordered that anyone who had died of the plague should be buried at night. But by August so many people had died that the funerals had to take place in the day-time, too, and new graveyards had to be made outside the City, for the churchyards were full. Another rule which had to be changed was the one which forbade anyone who had the plague, or who lived in a house where the plague was from ever leaving that house. On August 12th, the Lord Mayor ordered that everyone who was well should go indoors by 9 o'clock at nights and leave the streets clear, so that the sick people and those from the plague-stricken houses could get out for a walk and have some fresh air without meeting anyone else. By the last week in August, Pepys noted that over 6,000 people had died that week, and he felt sure that the number was really more than that.

Despite all his fears and sadness at this dreadful time, Pepys still enjoyed dressing-up in his good clothes and going out to dinner to meet those few friends who, like him, had stayed on in London. He also went to meetings in his parish to discuss with other important people what they could do to stop the plague from spreading and to try to stop people from coming in contact with it. They had one very sad case brought before them of a man who had broken the rule that no one should leave a house in which there was the plague, because he had smuggled out to a friend the only one of his children who was left alive out of his family. "Alderman Hooker told us it was the child of a very able citizen in Gracious Street, a saddler, who had buried all the rest of his children of the plague, and himself and wife being now shut up in despair of escaping, did desire only to save the life of this little child; and so prevailed to have it received stark-naked into the arms of a friend, who brought it, having put it into new fresh clothes, to Greenwich." Pepys and the other Justices were so touched by this story of the poor parents' attempt to save the life of their last child and the care they had taken not to let it carry out any infection in its clothes, that they agreed that the child should be allowed to stay out of its home.

Nothing seemed to stop the plague from spreading. The Lord Mayor ordered that fires should be burned in the streets in the hope that they would purify the air, and he forbade friends to attend funerals. In one day, however, Pepys saw forty or fifty people going along with three funerals, just the same as before the Lord Mayor's order. They even began to be careless about shutting-up the houses where there was plague, so that Pepys was much more afraid of meeting anyone. By the end of September, the numbers of dead began to fall a little, but "what a sad time it is to see no boats upon the river; and grass grows all up and down White Hall court and nobody but poor wretches in the streets." Everywhere he went he heard people talking about their friends who were sick or dead, and he heard that in Westminster there was not one doctor left alive and only one chemist still living.

By the end of November, the plague began to die down, and everyone hoped that the infection would end with the cold weather. Pepys' father wrote to him from the country to say that he had seen the waggon go up to London full of passengers once more, so evidently some Londoners were beginning to return home. By the end of December the plague was almost over. Early in January, 1666, Pepys was able to write how "delightful it is to see the town full of people again; and shops begin to open." It was February before the King and the Court returned to Whitehall, and even then the plague was not quite finished. Pepys continued to mention the plague from time to time, until another disaster overtook London later in the year.

THE FIRE

PEPYS and his wife had asked some friends to dinner on Sunday, September 2nd, 1666. The maids were up very late on the Saturday evening, getting everything ready for the next day, and while they were busy they saw the glow of a fire start in the sky. By 3 o'clock on the Sunday morning, its glow had become so bright that one of the maids, Jane, woke her master to see it. Pepys slipped on his dressing-gown and went to the window to watch it. It seemed fairly far away, so after a time he went back to bed. When he got up in the morning, it looked as though the fire was dying down, though he could still see some flames. So he set to work to tidy his room and put his things back where he wanted them after the maids had cleaned everything.

While he was doing this, Jane came in to say that she had heard that the fire was a bad one: three hundred houses had been burned down in the night and the fire was still burning. Pepys went out to see for himself. He went to the Tower of London and climbed up on a high part of the buildings so that he could see what was happening. From there, Pepys could see that it was, indeed, a bad fire and that even the houses on London Bridge were burning. The Lieutenant of the Tower told him that the fire had started in a baker's shop in Pudding Lane; the baker's house had caught fire from the over-heated oven and then the flames had quickly spread to the other houses in the narrow lane. Pepys took a boat to get nearer to the fire from the river. He watched people whose houses had been burned or were near the fire trying to get their furniture away by boats. Other poor people who had stayed in their houses as long as they dared, hoping against hope that the flames would not reach them, were running down the lanes to escape by the stone steps to the river. Even the pigeons, Pepys wrote later, seemed to stay on the houses as long as they could until the flames scorched their wings so that they could not fly away.

The fire was obviously spreading quickly up the rows of wooden houses and across the narrow lanes. Pepys was alarmed at the amount of damage that had been done already and the rate at which the fire was spreading, and he was worried because no one seemed to be doing anything to stop it. There was, in fact, little that could be done in those days. There were no fire brigades, and no means of putting out flames except for small water squirts and a supply of buckets which were sometimes kept in the parish church. Here is a water squirt and one of the buckets, with a fireman's helmet. You can imagine that these would not be much help against a really big fire.

The usual thing to do was to pull burning houses down by fixing long hooks on to the roofs; this was quite easy to do to timber houses and at least it helped to stop the fire from spreading to other houses. But Pepys could not see anyone doing even this, and so he decided to go on to Whitehall to tell the King and the Duke of York about the fire. They did not seem to have heard anything about it, but the King, when he heard Pepys' story, told him to go to the Lord Mayor "and command him to spare no houses, but to pull down before the fire every way."

So Pepys went back to the city, pushing his way past crowds of people carrying on their backs or in carts all they had been able to save from their houses, and sometimes meeting sick people being carried in their beds. Eventually he found the Lord Mayor in one of the streets looking "like a man spent, with a handkerchief about his neck." When Pepys told him of the King's message, the Lord Mayor said, "Lord! what can I do? I am spent: people will not obey me. I have been pulling down houses; but the fire overtakes us faster than we can do it." He said that he did not need the soldiers which the Duke of York said he might have to help him, and that he was going home to rest because he had been up all night.

Pepys went home, too, noticing as he walked along, that still no one seemed to be doing anything to stop the fire, and that it seemed to be growing worse. In fact, some warehouses with oil and wine and brandy in them had caught fire, so the blaze was fiercer than ever.

By the time he reached his own house, it was twelve o'clock and his friends had already arrived. They had a very good dinner and enjoyed it, but, of course they could talk of nothing but the fire. Pepys had planned that after dinner they should look at his new furniture and his books, but instead he set off with one of his guests to look at the fire once more. They found the streets packed with carts trying to get belongings away from houses near the fire, and the flames were spreading so quickly that Pepys saw that houses which had been taking in furniture for friends in the morning were having to move out their own furniture by the afternoon. He met the King and the Duke of York; they had come down by barge from Whitehall to see for themselves what was happening. Once again the King ordered that houses should be pulled down to stop the fire from spreading, but it was impossible to do this quickly enough.

Pepys then went home to join his wife and their other guests, and they all went on the river to watch the fire, and when the heat and the smoke became too unpleasant, they went to an ale-house on the other side of the river and watched from there until it was dark.

They "saw the fire grow; and, as it grew darker, appeared more and more; and in corners and upon steeples, and between churches and houses, as far as we could see up the hill of the City, in a most horrid, malicious, bloody flame, not like the fine flame of an ordinary fire . . We stayed till, it being darkish, we saw the fire as only one entire arch of fire from this to the other side the bridge, and in a bow up the hill for an arch of above a mile long: it made me weep to see it. The churches, houses, and all on fire, and flaming at once; and a horrid noise the flames made, and the cracking of houses at their ruin. So home with a sad heart, and there find everybody discoursing and lamenting the fire." They found Tom Hater, Pepys' clerk at the office, waiting for them to ask if he might stay with them because his own house had been burned.

Pepys and his wife became afraid that in time the flames would reach their house, too. They began to pack their goods, trying to decide what to save. It was almost impossible to get the use of a cart, for everybody was wanting one, but a neighbour had been lucky enough to get some and she offered one to Pepys. He was therefore able to get some of their "best things" away to a friend in the country. The note-books in which he had written up his diary so far were among the treasures that he made sure of saving in this way.

Pepys and his wife worked all through that night and for the next two days getting all the rest of their furniture and their goods away by river while there was still time to empty the house. At the end of it, they were completely exhausted: they had had no sleep and had not had time to eat a proper meal. One maid had left them to go home to help her mother, and Elizabeth was cross at being left with so much to do. Pepys dug two holes in the garden: in one he buried important naval papers from the office and some money chests, and in the other he put his favourite wine and cheese, in the hope that they would all be safe in the ground, even if the house did catch fire. When he had finished, he tried to write to his father, but the post-house, as he called it, had been burned down by then and so it was impossible to send any letters.

At 2 o'clock on the Wednesday morning, September 5th, Elizabeth wakened her husband to tell him that the fire had reached the bottom of their lane. He took her to a safe place in Woolwich, and left her there with a servant and some of their money, warning them never to leave the money unguarded. (It was £2,350 in gold!) He returned home, so certain that he would find the Navy Office and his house on fire when he reached it, that he dared not ask anyone for news. But when he reached Seething Lane, he found that all was safe. The Duke of York had been placed in charge of the city and the fire-fighting, and men had been brought up from the naval dockyards at Woolwich and Deptford to blow up houses. The noise had frightened people, but the gunpowder brought the houses down so that it was easier to quench the flames, and made gaps too big for the flames to leap across. So at last the fire was under control and was beginning to burn itself out. Pepys met some friends and together they walked round the streets to see the sights: they saw that whole streets had been destroyed, and the ground was so hot from the smouldering ashes that it burned their feet.

That night, some of the men from the dockyards stayed at the Navy Office, so Pepys was able to lie down to have a good sleep at last. He wrote in his diary: "it is a strange thing to see how long this time did look since Sunday, having been always full of variety of actions, and little sleep, that it looked like a week or more, and I had forgot almost the day of the week." It had, in fact, been little more than four days, though for many weeks more there were small fires as timber which was still smouldering burst into flames again. By the Friday, September 6th, the worst was over. Pepys realized how dirty he was from all the smoke and from the work he had done in clearing his house and his office, so he went out to try to buy a new shirt. Many of the shops had been burned down, and the stalls in Westminster Hall where Pepys usually bought his shirts had not been able to open because the Hall was piled high with goods from the houses which had been destroyed. In the end Pepys had to borrow a shirt from a friend.

This map shows you how much of London was burnt down.

Can you count up how many churches were in the burnt area, and either damaged or destroyed? In fact, you will see that very little of the City was left.

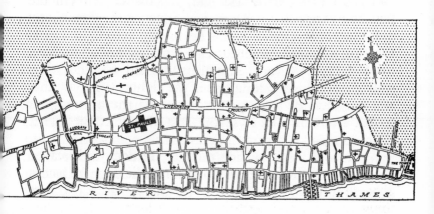

As the fires died down, everyone was trying to get in touch with their friends to find out what had happened to them. Whenever people met, they discussed why the fire had broken out and how it had spread so quickly. Some thought that it was a punishment from God; others thought that it must be the work of foreigners or of Roman Catholics. It had been such a terrible fire that many found it hard to believe the truth—that it was, in fact, a fire that had started in a perfectly ordinary way from the baker's oven in Pudding Lane.

Those who had been lucky enough to escape began to get their belongings back into their houses. One of the first things Pepys did when he got his books back was to write up an account of the fire in his diary. By September 14th, he had the carpenters in the house putting up the beds again, and he got workmen in the garden to dig up the naval papers, and his wine and cheese (though he was careful not to let them see that there was some money hidden there, too). By September 22nd, everything was straight again: Pepys said that he had never seen his house look so clean before. He had, indeed, been fortunate. He had lost neither home nor office, and with all the upheaval and removal of his belongings he found that he had lost nothing except for two pictures. For a long time afterwards, however, he often had nightmares about fires and about houses falling down.

London, was "a sad sight", Pepys thought one morning as he went down by river and saw all the ruined houses. Thousands of the people were homeless and they had to camp in the fields outside the city. Luckily the weather was fine. The King ordered the districts around London to send in food, for otherwise the unfortunate Londoners might have starved, too.

When the City Surveyors came to check the damage, they found that thirteen thousand houses had been destroyed in four hundred streets, and that almost ninety churches had been destroyed or were so badly damaged that they would have to be pulled down for safety. Only about a sixth of the city was left unharmed.

Few people had lost their lives, for there had been time to get away from the fire, but everyone whose house had been burned was in a sad plight. Families had lost their homes and some had not been able to save any of their clothes or their furniture: merchants had lost all their stocks as well as their premises. There was no insurance then, and no one knew how they were going to be able to build their houses or start their businesses again. In fact, we do not know how so many of them were able to afford to rebuild their houses or reopen their shops. There must have been many like Pepys who were able to hide their money or get it away to a place of safety.

There were many plans for the rebuilding of London. Sir Christopher Wren, John Evelyn and Robert Hooke were only some of the famous men of the day who suggested that the chance should be taken to replan the city completely and to lay out new wide streets, but no one could afford to do much, and everyone was anxious to build his own house as quickly as possible. In the end, very little was done about replanning the streets.

The King appointed a Court of Fire Judges to decide disputes about burned property. If the landlord could not afford to rebuild the house or shop, then the tenant was allowed to do this and was given a reduced rent in return for doing so: if the owner could afford to rebuild, then he was allowed to charge more rent to help to cover some of the expense. The judges were so fair that everyone accepted their decisions as being the best possible ones. Because the fire had shown how dangerous it was to have a town built of timber houses, it was ordered that in future every new house had to be of brick or stone.

Here is one of these houses built after the Fire:

And so gradually a new London came to replace the city that had been burned down in that dreadful week. A tax was put on coal to raise funds to help the rebuilding, and with that money the City Council was able to afford to widen a few streets and to replace about half the churches that had been burnt down. Not every house that had been destroyed was rebuilt: because the new brick houses were bigger than some of the old wooden ones, it is thought that about nine thousand houses were built to replace the thirteen thousand houses destroyed.

Many of the well-to-do merchants who had had to find new houses in the country outside London because of the fire, liked it so much that they did not come back to live in London, so not so many houses were needed. The new houses which were built were plain brick buildings two, three, or four storeys high according to the width of the street they were built in and the wealth of the owner. They were rebuilt one by one as the surveyors marked out the site again after the rubble had been cleared away.

The Fire gave Sir Christopher Wren his great chance. His plans for a new city were not accepted, and he did not build many of the private houses, but he was given the task of designing most of the churches which were re-built. He built St. Paul's Cathedral as we know it today:

He also rebuilt many of the famous London churches like St. Mary-le-Bow in Cheapside and St. Bride's in Fleet Street, whose beautiful spire this is.

Wren chose a new style for his great cathedral and his churches. He did not rebuild in the Gothic or medieval style of the churches which had been burned, but he got his ideas from the great Renaissance buildings in Italy where, since the sixteenth century, architects had been using again the style of the ancient Greek and Roman buildings. The windows and arches of Wren's churches are wide and rounded, and the porches and all the decoration on the steeples are of classical pillars and ornaments. Though it is easy to recognize Wren's work, he managed to give each of the fifty-one churches he built a style all its own; the steeples are particularly lovely, for Wren knew that in the crowded city it would be the steeples that men would notice most about his churches.

Here are some of the spires of Wren's churches:

Wren may also have helped Robert Hooke, the City Surveyor, to design the Monument, which still stands today near to the place where the Fire started. The inscription on the Monument says that the City was rebuilt in three years. In actual fact, it was at least twenty years before most of the city was rebuilt. It was 1696 before the surveyors had finished marking out all the sites, and it was 1710 before Sir Christopher Wren, then 78 years of age, saw his son put the last stone on the highest point of St. Paul's Cathedral. Even this was a great achievement when we think of all their difficulties.

In many ways, the Great Fire of 1666 was a blessing in disguise for London. It cleared away the old plague-ridden houses and gave Londoners the chance to build better houses and clearer streets, and to improve the water supply and the drainage. Perhaps, too, it was fortunate that the men of Pepys' London were not able to afford the magnificent plans which men like Wren and Evelyn had for a completely new city. If they had been able to do so, we should have had a London with much wider and finer streets than it has today. But because Londoners built their houses on nearly the same sites as before, the streets of medieval and Elizabethan London have come down to us. Some of the tiny streets in the City today, like Milk Street and Bread Street, are a great nuisance to modern traffic, but at least they let us know the size of the medieval streets and their names tell us what used to be sold there, even though none of the actual houses and few of the churches have survived because of the Great Fire of London in 1666.

THE END OF THE DIARY

ON MAY 5th, 1664, Pepys noticed for the first time that his eyes were beginning "every day to grow less and less able to bear with long reading or writing, though it be by daylight; which I never observed till now." By 1667 he was often referring to his eyes; how much they hurt him and how hard he found it to read or write for any length of time. He got a pair of spectacles which sound rather strange: they had two tubes with glass in for each eye, and magnified writing for him. His doctor gave him some medicine to take and some drops to put in his eyes.

Nothing really helped him. At last, he had to ask for leave of absence from his office so that he could take a long holiday in the hope that that would rest his eyes. On May 31st, 1669, he worked late in his office to finish off his work before he left, and then Elizabeth and he went out to say goodbye to some friends. When they got back home at night, Pepys very sadly wrote the last sentences in his diary. "And thus ends all that I doubt I shall ever be able to do with my own eyes in the keeping of my Journal, I being not able to do it any longer, having done now so long as to undo my eyes almost every time I take a pen in my hand: and, therefore, whatever comes of it, I must forbear."

Pepys' eyes were a little better after his holiday, and he was able to go on with his work until he retired in 1688, although he could no longer do much writing for himself. When he died on May 26th, 1703, he left all his books to his nephew, but he asked that afterwards they should go to his old College in Cambridge. His books are in the library of Magdalene College, Cambridge, to this day: they are even in the very bookcases which he bought for them in 1666. And in among all his books are the six note-books, bound in leather, in which he kept his diary.

THINGS TO DO

THERE are many books about the seventeenth century which will help you to understand more about the times in which Pepys wrote his diary. These are only some of the books which you will probably find in your school library or in your public library :

> Dorothy Hartley and Margaret M. Elliot : *Life and work of the people of England: the seventeenth century.* Batsford.
>
> M. Harrison and A. A. M. Wells. *Picture source book for social history in the seventeenth century.* Allen and Unwin.
>
> Historical Association : ed. E. S. de Beer : *English history in pictures. Stuart times.* George Philip and Son.
>
> M. and C. H. B. Quennell : *History of Everyday things in England,* vol. 2. Batsford.
>
> G. M. Trevelyan : *Illustrated English social history,* vol 2. Longmans.

Most libraries have an edition of Pepys' Diary. Read some of it for yourself, for example, the entries between June 7th and December 31st, 1665, when the plague was at its worst, and for September, 1666, when Pepys was writing about the Great Fire and the damage that it did.

As you read the Diary and this book, keep a diary of your own. Imagine that you are living in London in the 1660s, and that you know Pepys and his wife. Perhaps you work with him at the Navy Office and he often asks you to go out with him to see the sights. Perhaps he takes you home with him to see something that he has bought for the house—which is exactly what he would have done had he known you. Or perhaps you are a friend of Elizabeth and she talks to you about her husband when you visit her.

THINGS TO DO IN A GROUP

TRY to find out more about the kind of house Pepys lived in and how all the different rooms were furnished. Keep a book in which you write your descriptions and put in illustrations. Make up a big wall picture of the different rooms, or make a model out of boxes, with your drawings of the furniture mounted on cardboard to furnish the rooms. Visit any museum near you or any of the big houses open to the public in your district where you might see similar furniture. Our drawings come from the Victoria and Albert Museum and the Geffrye Museum in London.

Find out more about the costume of the time, and make up a book of your descriptions and drawings. Not many of the costumes of this period have survived in museums, and there are not many English portraits of this time which show a full length figure, so you will have to use a book such as C. W. and P. Cunnington: *Handbook of English costume in the seventeenth century* (Faber and Faber) to show you what we think they were like. Dress wire or cardboard figures so that they can go into the model house, or paste your drawings on to a wall picture of the house or on to a street frieze of London.

Listen to records of the instruments that Pepys liked to play, for example, the records issued by Columbia in their *History of Music series*, period 1, and by Decca in their *Early English Keyboard Music*. Perhaps your music teacher will help you to sing ' Greensleeves ' and ' Barbara Allan ', and teach you Pepys' own song, ' Beauty Retire '. It is in Sir Frank Bridge's book, *Samuel Pepys, lover of musique*. Try to see some of the instruments in a museum or in a house open to the public, and make up a book of descriptions and drawings of them.

Find out more about the ships of the Navy in Pepys' day. See if there are any models or paintings of these ships in your museum or art gallery: ours came from the Science Museum in London and the Queen's House, the Maritime Museum, Greenwich. Make a book of your own about how the ships were rigged, how they were steered, etc., and mount your pictures to make up a frieze of a scene at sea.

Learn more about the ways in which people travelled in Pepys' days, and write accounts of them. Draw pictures to paste on to the wall frieze of the street scene, or put them on cardboard to stand in front of it.

Make wall friezes of what a street in London must have looked like before and after the Great Fire. See if you have any medieval houses and churches in your town to help you to get the houses right before the Fire, and see if you can find some houses and churches built in the late seventeenth or early eighteenth century so that you can understand better the sort of houses and churches that were rebuilt in London after the Fire. Make a scrap book of pictures and drawings of different periods so that you can learn to recognize the styles of architecture. If you live in a town which had a fire at some period and was rebuilt, or live in a district which was bombed so that your Council is having to decide what to rebuild, try to find out about the plans for doing this.

Paint a big wall picture of the Fire of London, and write accounts of it. If you are in London, go to see the diorama in the London Museum at Kensington Palace.

If you live in London, or visit it at any time for a holiday or on a school visit, try to see the part which Pepys knew and imagine what it must have been like in his day. Go to Tower Hill station by Underground. As you leave the station you will see the Church of All Hallows, Barking, immediately in front of you, and the Tower of London is very near. Turn right, out of the station, and take the first turn to the right, and you will be in Seething Lane. The Navy Office was on the right hand side of the lane, where the gardens in front of the Port of London Authority buildings are now, and the Church of St. Olave's, where Pepys and his wife went to church and where they are buried, is at the top of the lane. Come back down the lane and turn right along Great Tower Street and Eastcheap, and you will see many of the little lanes where Pepys used to wander. One lane on the left-hand side, Lovat Lane, still has its cobbles with the gutter running down the middle, and it is easy to picture what it must have looked like when it had overhanging houses. A little further on is Pudding Lane where the Fire started, and at the bottom of it is the Monument to the Fire. St. Paul's Cathedral is only a short walk further on from there. If you live too far away from London to do this, there is a film-strip by Common Ground called 'Pepys' London' which your teacher might be able to show you.

GLOSSARY

This is a list of special words. If the word you want to know is not here, look for it in your dictionary.

cassock: a long close-fitting coat.

Commonwealth: the government of England between 1649 and 1660 when there was no King, and the country was ruled by Cromwell and the army.

cordage: the ropes of the rigging of a ship.

faggot: a bundle of wood.

pennants: the long pointed streamers flown from a ship.

press gangs: a group of sailors, under an officer, who went ashore and forced men to join their ship.

serge: a strong woollen material.

stuff: a woollen material.

tabby: a silk material, sometimes with a strip of another colour in it, but more often with a wavy mark in it of the same colour.

tapestry, -ies: a fabric painted, embroidered or woven with colours and used for hangings and curtains.

vest: a collarless and sleeveless garment worn below a coat. (It has become our waistcoat.)